After the Darkness: Reflections on the Holocaust is produced by becker&mayer!, Bellevue, Washington.
www.beckermayer.com

Design: Katie LeClercq
Editorial: Marcie DiPietro
Image Research: Shayna Ian
Production Coordination: Cindy Curren

Library of Congress Cataloging-in-Publication Data
Wiesel, Elie, 1928-
After the darkness: reflections on the Holocaust / Elie Wiesel.
p. cm.
ISBN 0-8052-4182-5
1. Holocaust, Jewish (1939-1945) I. Title.
D804.3 .W465 2002
940.53'18—dc21

www.schocken.com

Printed in China

First Edition
9 8 7 6 5 4 3 2 1

Four hundred liberated Jewish youth, including Elie Wiesel, ride to freedom from Buchenwald to France, June 1945. (front cover)

This mountain of shoes was found in the concentration camp at Majdanek, Poland, after its liberation. (previous page)

Personal belongings of Jewish prisoners at Chelmno, Poland, cover the floor of a nearby synagogue. (right)

Reflections on the Holocaust

Elie Wiesel

Translated from the French by Benjamin Moser

After the Darkness

Schocken Books
New York

BACK THEN, the dark side of the human heart took over most of Europe. In the name of racial purity and absolute power, it turned hatred and violence into hungry gods eager for blood and death. The Nazis changed the world forever, but as hard as they tried to stamp out Jewish life, they couldn't.

The Nazis' reign lasted twelve years, from 1933 to 1945. It ended only when their opponents, fighting a just and noble war, forced the Nazis' military and ideological leaders to surrender—in shame but not in remorse.

Whose fault was it? Just Adolf Hitler's? Just those people who gave in to his tyranny? Just those whose hatred of democracy was so strong that they finally managed to smother it? Seven months after Hitler took power, the concentration camp at Dachau opened its gates to his political opponents. Soon, it was the Jews' turn. During the Nazi era, in thousands of towns and cities, men and women—young and old, from all walks of life—would eventually find themselves, from one day to the next, barricaded and condemned, simply because their community recalled an ancient covenant with God: the Jewish people.

Their unique ordeal, their incomparable torment bears a name that one hopes will make people tremble, tomorrow and forever more: the Holocaust.

This term, from the Latin word *holocaustum*, means "burnt offering." Most people accept it to describe these horrible events. Some people, however, are troubled by its evocation of a religious act: it would be wrong, they reason, to lend the event any purifying value. The truth is that it's an inappropriate word because no word can express this tragedy: no word can contain the humiliation, the suffering, and the loss of human life that it is meant to encompass. We use it only because we can do no better.

The greatest writers are incapable of describing what the Holocaust means. How to explain or even describe the agony, the terror, the prayers, the tears, the tenderness, the sadness of the scientifically prepared death of six million human beings? Six million young and old, rich and poor, scholarly and illiterate, strong and weak, religious and atheistic people. Six million human beings sentenced to death by an evil dictatorship not because of their faith or their circumstances but because of their very being.

When we talk about the "Holocaust," we mean the destruction of a third of the Jewish people. Who could have imagined it?

Until Hitler stepped onto the world stage, Jews had lived more or less peacefully, although things were

certainly better in western Europe than in central and eastern Europe. In France, for example, even though there was a long-standing tradition of anti-Semitism among many of its people, Jews could assimilate but didn't have to. Many people, both in private life and in the government, were influenced by the emancipation of the French Jews that dated back to Napoleon's time. In medicine and in politics, in business and in higher learning, Jews had no need to lie about their background. Everyone knew that Léon Blum, prime minister, or Henri Bergson, the famous philosopher, was Jewish.

The situation in eastern Europe was more worrisome. Throughout modern history, pogroms had periodically brought death and destruction to the Jews. By the middle of the twentieth century—in Poland, in Hungary, in Romania—Jews were subject to strict quotas in universities and government posts. And the influential pro-Nazi fascist parties stirred up local citizens, accusing the Jews of being the eternal enemies of Christ and the State, hateful myths that had endured.

Long used to suffering and challenges, Jews had learned to live with adversity. Despite the dangers all around them, they built homes, created schools, and organized religious and cultural institutions. So hoodlums pulled out their beards in the streets. Well, observant Jews would just have to be a little more careful. So anti-Semitic newspapers spewed hate. Well, eventually they'd get bored. In the meantime, people had to earn a living so they could educate their children. Even the poorest families saved what pennies they could to pay teachers what they deserved; learning was hope. In little Jewish villages, a wise man was a prince, respected by everyone, the pride of the community.

So many memoirs, survivors' testimonies, describe what life was like before. The authors vividly recall their childhood, their world of nostalgia and melancholy. It is not a paradise lost they're mourning. Everyone had troubles, fears, sorrows. But in pre-Holocaust Europe, they had their parents, their friends, their lives. Tomorrow was filled with worries, but it was also charged with promise. Too often, alas, it would be promise unfulfilled, unfulfillable.

1. Three Jewish women in Poland enjoy each other's company, 1938.

2. A young Yugoslavian boy poses on his family's car, 1939.

3. First-graders study their lessons at a public school in Hamburg, 1933.

3.

THE MAN WRITING these lines must be frank: he doesn't want to tell you about this uniquely bloody and murderous period; he's reluctant to talk about his past. What can he achieve by making you sad? Why keep denouncing the indifference of some and the collaboration of others? And why bring up his own past when millions of other human beings have suffered as much as—if not more than—he has?

And yet . . . .

The survivor must be a witness. He doesn't have the right to hide behind a facade of false modesty. The easy way would be just to say nothing—but it's been a long time since he took the easy way.

So listen. Listen to the haunted memories of a Jewish child from a little Carpathian village.

I was happy at home in the way only a child full of love and curiosity can be. I was happy because my family had a house. And because in that house I had my parents and my three sisters. I was happy because I loved them. And because they loved me.

My grandfather had served as a stretcher-bearer in the Austro-Hungarian army during World War I, and had fallen on the battlefield. He left behind a widow, still young, who, along with her oldest son, my father, ran a little grocery store. My grandmother worked the cash register. I remember her: pale, thin, discreet, she spoke little, and softly. All she did was pray, except when speaking to her grandchildren. One wretched day, before getting into a sealed wagon that was to carry us away, she put on her shroud. She was the only one who saw that we were setting out on a journey toward death.

But until that day, in our little town, we were a happy, peaceful family, in a town like any other: we were afraid of crime and poverty, and complained only about idleness.

The young respected the old. Teenagers played soccer in the park. Some people joined Zionist or Communist groups. The Zionists dreamed of a Jewish national rebirth; the Communists, of worldwide revolution. Here and there, people fell in love, loves that, according to the circumstances, would blossom or die.

I went to school. I studied the Bible, the Talmud, and their commentaries. I was eager to learn, to deepen my faith. I believed in the Eternal One and held fast His laws. My whole soul

Three sisters enjoy a snack in the doorway of their mother's store in Poland, 1934.

awaited the arrival of the Messiah, who would make people instruments of peace, not violence. I was not the only one who spent my time in study and meditation. The Yeshiva, the Talmud school, was always full, as were the many synagogues.

Like most Jewish villages (called *shtetls*), life in mine revolved around the laws and precepts of the Jewish religion. We happily observed the Sabbath and the holidays. We respected our traditions: we invited strangers to eat with us, we were generous to beggars, we never left a sick person alone in the hospital, we never turned away an anonymous wanderer. This was true of all the Jewish communities, large and small. Shared aims connected them. This was their common heritage. And their hope. The rest was less important. Hate? We got used to it. Persecution too.

Then, suddenly, the earth began quaking under our feet. Illusions, beliefs, structures collapsed. It was an awful exile we were to begin. Expulsed, evicted, the unexpected became the norm: families were separated; parents were humiliated, unable to protect or come to the aid of their sick or hungry children. Rich people were made poor in an instant. Influential people were stripped of their power. No one was left at home, and our destination was unknown. It struck everyone who wasn't Aryan, who wasn't German. It was like a Biblical plague was assailing the most vulnerable of the European peoples. The most ancient, too. And surely the most wronged.

Were Jews the only victims of German Nazism? There were others, of course—in war actions and in the concentration camps. Polish, Russian, French, and Dutch people; Gypsies and gay people; people who resisted Nazism. But if not all the victims were Jews, only the Jews were all victims.

A Zionist youth group meets in Czechoslovakia, 1932.

OF COURSE, this journey back to a time of hatred and absurdity must start at the beginning. But where to begin? After all, hatred isn't a recent creation: it's as old as the human race. Death entered history with the murder of a man by his brother.

Persecutions, massacres, mutilations, rapes, burnings: was it not hatred that inspired and justified them? Ancient religious hatreds, fickle economic hatreds, hidden social hatreds, open racist hatreds: Nazi and fascist ideologies were certainly encouraged by these hatreds, but the Germans added new elements that were entirely their own.

Even though it was rooted in history, the Holocaust went beyond history.

And we need to name the person who was its center, if not its incarnation: Adolf Hitler.

This failed painter, a former Austrian corporal wounded in World War I, will be remembered as the leader who pushed humanity over the edge: the *evil genius* of the worst of all conflicts, of all ideological battles, of all war crimes.

Those two words sum him up perfectly: he was drawn to evil and served it with genius. Even his enemies recognized his unmatched skill for taking advantage of the angry undercurrents of resentment felt by untold numbers of Germans who believed themselves to have been unfairly defeated in the war and mistreated in its aftermath; he turned them into agents of his fanaticism. Like Alexander the Great and Genghis Khan, but more cruel, he rallied them to conquer distant lands and dominate their peoples; his slogan: "Today Germany, tomorrow the world."

Not many people took him seriously at first. Nor did they worry much about the nasty program he outlined in his *Mein Kampf.* Written while he was in prison after the collapse of his 1923 insurrection in Munich against the government, the book described everything he would do after he took power. Most people considered the Munich coup insignificant. The German people are so civilized, so proud of their great artists—Goethe, Schiller, Kant, Heine. There was no way they were about to let themselves be manipulated by a wretched petty tyrant who couldn't get over the pathetic social failures of his early life.

But amid the economic wreckage Kaiser Wilhelm's delusions of grandeur and a lost war had left behind, Hitler's rants found sympathetic ears and open hearts, and minds that could be swayed.

The problem was that the Weimar Republic, the democratic government that emerged from the postwar chaos in Germany, couldn't manage to solve the country's basic economic problems. Every day brought more unemployment and a currency that constantly declined in value. Just to buy some bread or vegetables, you needed a big bag packed full of bills. This tired and hungry people, not surprisingly, was unhappy. The Nazis promised them pride, and prosperity, and revenge.

After he became the all-powerful chancellor in January 1933, Hitler even managed to fool the leaders of the great democracies themselves. They finally caved in to his territorial demands (he described every one as "the last"). The German army occupied the Rhineland, Austria, and Czechoslovakia without real opposition from the major European powers, France and Great Britain, who scrapped their mutual defense agreement with Czechoslovakia—betraying their courageous little ally at a shameful conference in Munich in November 1938.

Ethnic German recruits to the German Army swear allegiance to the Führer.

1933 "I saw my world starting to crumble"

Adolf Hitler, having obtained German citizenship, reached the first plateau in his quest for absolute power on January 30, 1933. On that fateful day, after much political manipulation, President Von Hindenburg, an old and senile man, appointed Hitler to be Chancellor of Germany. This, at first, did not have a particular impact on anyone's life. Although more and more Brownshirts became visible, they were not considered as a political power but as a bunch of rowdies and bullies. It was the general consensus that the Hitler regime would be over before it could take a strong foothold. After all, less than 50 percent of the German people had voted for the Nazi Party as of March 1933. It could not have been foreseen that Adolf Hitler would make dead sure that this would be the last free election in Germany for a long time to come. One did not want to allow a vague sense of fear to surface and everyone tried to have a positive attitude. Once that false sense of security began to crack, life for the European Jew would never be the same.

The letter came in the spring of 1933, a few days before I was to turn nineteen. I saw my world starting to crumble. The letter informed me that my membership in the UVF [a sports club] had been terminated and that I was no longer welcome there. Forgotten the good times we had together, forgotten the many medals I had won for them, forgotten the camaraderie.

Having been an equal for all this time, how could it be possible that I had been declared a leper almost overnight? It was of no consolation that this was happening all over Germany, and only trying to convince myself that all this would be temporary let me cope with this cruel blow. This glimmer of hope was supported by a letter from the University in Berlin to whom I had written that I was Jewish and was it wise, under the circumstances, to start my studies there in the spring semester. The University wrote back, saying literally that it would be best if I waited "until this thing blows over." It was hard to stay optimistic and to think that I was just marking time and that, before long, I would be able to go on with my life as planned.

Margaret Lambert, born 1914, Germany

Then came Poland. At first, Hitler demanded the city of Danzig and its access to the sea. Supported by its Western allies, the Polish government refused to discuss it. Was this a reason to go to war? In France, public opinion wasn't so sure, not even the right wing. The Fascist-leaning writer Marcel Déat wrote: "Is it worth dying for Danzig?" But the official line from their Western allies was just what the Poles wanted to hear: there would be no more Munichs. France and Great Britain wouldn't abandon any more countries joined to them by strong ties of friendship and security. They would go to war to defend Poland.

But Hitler was soon to enjoy his first military victory, thanks to his new ally—Josef Stalin.

The nonaggression pact between these two dictators rocked the world like a global earthquake. The geopolitical map of Europe had been transformed with one swoop. The heavily armed Wehrmacht, the German army, was free to attack Poland without worrying about a Soviet counterattack. The pathetically naïve Polish military leaders, completely underestimating the invader's technical and numerical supremacy, boasted that they could quickly push the Germans all the way back to Berlin. But Poland's proud horsemen were plowed beneath the oncoming tanks; the German air force dominated their skies. Six weeks later, despite its badly equipped army's heroic defense, the Polish government surrendered.

For the three million Polish Jews, it was the beginning of the time of despair. The trap was soon going to close around them.

Up until then, Hitler's anti-Semitism seemed to have limited goals. His loathing of Jews was unsurpassed in the long history of anti-Semitism. But his intense hatred seemed to be directed toward Jewish influence, not the very existence of Jews themselves. He simply had in mind the gradual creation of a Germany without Jews—nothing more, but nothing less. He saw them as a dead weight, a curse, a cancer that threatened the health and survival of the German nation. This was the rationale for the Nuremberg Laws of September 1935.

At first, Jews were excluded from all areas of German life: from business, intellectual, and social life. The infamous laws forbade any familial, sexual, or professional contact between Jews and Germans. Jews were forbidden to go to plays or movies; forbidden to use public transportation; forbidden to go into parks; forbidden to own radios or bicycles. These measures were meant to make life unlivable for Jews; the Nazis hoped thereby to force Jews to leave Germany.

Those who wanted to emigrate could do so without too many bureaucratic delays, as long as they had a visa from a country that would take them. Great scientific, cultural, and

Hitler Youth stand at attention during a rally.

economic leaders were able to leave—Albert Einstein, Stefan Zweig (from Austria), Bertolt Brecht, Kurt Weill, Franz Werfel, and Sigmund Warburg were among those lucky enough to make it to London, Paris, Amsterdam, or New York. A visa could free a prisoner in Dachau or Buchenwald. But for the average citizen, emigration was harder: the free world didn't want them. The International Conference in Evian, France, in 1938 made that clear. The conference, organized purportedly to help German and Austrian refugees, instead provided rich entertainment for readers of Nazi newspapers. The eloquent participants explained the reasons why their governments couldn't host potential emigrants. Joseph Goebbels, Hitler's chief propagandist, chuckled in public, as if to say: Look at all these hypocritical countries berating us for not wanting to live with Jews! They are supposedly so generous and charitable, but how are they different from us?

On this shameful point he was absolutely right.

In the fall of 1938, the German Jews—even those who thought they would ride out the hideous storm raging around them—stepped up their efforts to leave Germany. This was the consequence of the notorious Kristallnacht, the "Night of the Broken Glass," on November 8-9. After an uprooted young Jew, Herschel Grynszpan, assassinated the German diplomat Ernst vom Rath in Paris, an official pogrom was unleashed across the nation. Hundreds of synagogues were burned; countless stores were looted; prominent members of the community were imprisoned. The Jews' fear now turned into panic.

A few months later, about a thousand Jewish emigrants with Cuban visas boarded the German steamship *Saint-Louis* in the port of Hamburg. Once they got to their destination, the Cuban authorities refused to let them land: their visas had been canceled.

Newspapers throughout the world reported on the unfortunate passengers. As the boat sailed through American territorial waters, people hoped that President Franklin Roosevelt, known for his benevolence, would grant them asylum. After these Jews had so miraculously escaped the horrors of Kristallnacht and endured the hardship of their Atlantic crossing, how could anyone send them back to Germany? Yet the boat headed back to Europe. Some more generous western European countries—especially France, Holland, and Great Britain—finally let the refugees in.

The Nazis cheered.

Since it was now clear that no one would take in the remaining Jews of Germany, the Nazis revised their plans. On June 22, 1940, after the surrender of France, Hitler, his generals, and his Italian ally Benito Mussolini talked about occupying Madagascar and making it a kind of gigantic ghetto for European Jews. Hitler went so far as to name a local governor for Madagascar, a *Gauleiter*—in this case a fanatic Nazi by the name of Philip Bouhler, who was famous for his brutality. The Führer dropped the idea, however, to devote himself to preparations for Operation Barbarossa—the invasion of the Soviet Union.

In the meantime, Adolf Eichmann, a high-ranking officer of the SS, the Nazis' elite military unit, was charged with helping Jews emigrate at any price, even by kicking them out illegally.

The Germans changed their policy when they occupied Poland, the Netherlands, Belgium, France, and later the Baltic countries and vast areas of the Soviet Union. Elimination gave way to extermination.

The Essenweinstrasse synagogue in Nuremberg stands in ruins following the devastation of Kristallnacht.

1938 "A sight I will never forget"

Everything changed on the 9th and 10th of November 1938. We had gone to school as usual in the morning and, upon arrival, were immediately sent home without explanation. We were on our way to the Bellevue Station where we lived when the train suddenly slowed as we passed a sight I will never forget. What we saw was the fancy Fassanenstrasse synagogue in flames. The police and firemen were out in force, but just stood there and watched, not making any attempt to stop the flames. We found out later that they were there to prevent the flames from spreading to nearby buildings. It was such a shock that I was unable to speak. I had to do something to stop that icy fear. Doing something translated into writing. I opened my backpack, the poetry reader was on top. I opened it at random and read Goethe's famous line *Edel sei der Mensch hilfreich und gut* (Man should be noble, helpful, and good). I wrote next to that line: *Goethe bid "man" to be good. What is happening to us? What is happening in our Deutschland, our country which Opa is so proud of, which Papa has fought and suffered for?*

When I got home, Mama kept asking where Papa was as though any of us would come up with the answer. We could see the smoke of our synagogue in the Lefkowitzstrasse burning. We could also hear the smashing of glass and the sound of screaming and sirens. Hitler Youth were marching to the beat of drums singing *Wenn das Judenblut vom Messer sprizt* (When Jewish blood splashes from the knife). Mama, Bibi, Tante Hans and I held on to each other and waited. It was late in the afternoon and already dark when Papa appeared. We heard his familiar steps on the stairs. Joy replaced fear. Being together was all that mattered. *Bitte, bitte lieber Gott*, I prayed, looking at the ceiling. *Let us get through this night.*

Eve Nussbaum Soumerai, born 1926, Germany

GENERAL REINHARD HEYDRICH, head of German security services, had already been planning the extermination before September 1939 when the invasion of Poland began. Before Poland had been completely subdued, he circulated a top-secret order to the leaders of the Gestapo—the German secret police—and the SS. In it, he instructed them to round up the Jews in the invaded areas. They were to be placed in ghettos near important railroad junctions. Heydrich was clear: as many Jews as possible needed to be arrested.

During the sudden, devastating invasion of the Soviet Union that soon followed, still following Heydrich's orders, the SS-Einsatzgruppen, special units who had been active in Poland killing Jews and partisans, were now expanded and put to the task in an accelerated fashion. Charged with executing the Führer's will, they were to do away with the Jews in the newly occupied countries of eastern Europe.

The German authorities didn't talk about the "final solution to the Jewish question" yet—they would only make that decision in January 1942—but they were already carrying it out.

There were four Einsatzgruppen. Each—A, B, C, D— contained nine hundred SS soldiers and officers. They followed the four main Wehrmacht armies—on whom they depended for provisions and logistic support—as they advanced deep into the Soviet Union. Each SS group strove to outshine the others. Their statistics, constantly and precisely updated, proved it.

Vilnius and Minsk, Kiev and Kharkov, Berditchev and Zhytomyr—the same apocalyptic scenes were repeated everywhere. Spurred on by local anti-Semites, pogroms erupted in Jewish neighborhoods, spreading panic. In some places, the Germans locked the Jews into their synagogues and set them on fire. In other places, they led them into the forest and made them dig their own graves. The naked victims, killed by gunfire, fell over the edge on top of their dead neighbors. More than a million people died this way. Completely bewildered, perhaps unable to believe what was happening, the victims stepped forward, sometimes family by family, sometimes line by line, to the edge of the ditch. Few, very few, escaped. Some victims at Babi-Yar or Ponàr were wounded but not killed; they were protected by the dead bodies on top of them. After nightfall, they managed to crawl to the surface—some only to be caught soon afterward. Others, however, very few, found places to hide, and survived.

Later, they would tell their stories. The cruelty of the murderers. The numbness of the doomed. The hallucinating calm of the living dead. Adults didn't try to resist or escape. Old people didn't complain. Children didn't cry. One photo taken by a German soldier shows a father pointing out the sky to his little boy as they walked to their deaths. I wonder—I'll wonder for the rest of my life—what it was he wanted to show him.

Jews line up for roll call at Buchenwald, following their arrest during Kristallnacht.

1939 "We were young and willing to take chances"

From my aunt's house, knowing that the German troops were very close, my mother, some friends, and I fled further on foot. We traveled day and night, through forests and roads, until we saw the red sky in the distance and heard sounds coming from the battlefield. Realizing that the Germans were now in front of us, we turned around and went back home to Bendzin, where we were reunited with my father and sisters.

Upon our return, we were shocked to discover that, in the short time we were gone, the synagogue had been burned by the Germans. The surrounding old community of Jewish homes was also in ashes. Our apartment building and the rest of Bendzin had not been damaged.

In the first few weeks of German occupation, a series of restrictions were imposed on the Jewish population. Laws were passed to close libraries, sport clubs, movie houses, Jewish theaters, newspapers, etc. Youth movements were banned. All Jews were forced to wear a white armband with a blue Jewish star on it. Gathering in groups of more than six was forbidden.

Jews were not allowed to enter parks or use the main streets in town. Cars were confiscated from the few families that owned them in Bendzin. We were no longer allowed to ride the trains. At first we were permitted to stand on the streetcar platform, but that "privilege" soon ended. Factories and stores were taken over by the German commissioners, and Jewish owners were forced to work for the Germans and teach them how to operate their businesses.

The Jewish school did not open in September of 1939, nor ever again....

My father lost his job in the brewery. In order to earn some money for food, my father and I risked our lives by illegally taking the train (without wearing armbands) and trading smuggled goods in nearby cities....

I also helped my aunt by delivering meat that she was able to obtain on the black market. One time, my sister Hania and I took a train in order to trade some goods between Jedrzejow and Bendzin. We were young and willing to take chances, not realizing how great a risk we were taking. Many young people lost their lives, as we later found out, doing this sort of thing.

Jane Lipski [Jadzia Szpigelman],
born 1924, Poland

BY THIS TIME, the ghettos in Poland had long since become a fact of life. This strange word—"ghetto"—comes from medieval Italy, where it designated neighborhoods set aside for the Jews. Legend has it the ghetto of Venice was the first. Other cities followed its example. But no ancient ghetto knew the terror and suffering of the ghettos under Hitler.

The Germans used the same method everywhere. It depended as much on psychological brutality as on police cruelty to destabilize and demoralize the already vulnerable Jews. It aimed to separate them from the rest of the population, and to sever them from their customs, their traditions—everything familiar in their world. By imposing curfews, by requiring them to affix a yellow star to their clothing, by evicting them from their homes, by closing their shops and schools and confiscating their cherished belongings, the Nazis turned the Jews into targets of opportunity for their old enemies, as well as for their recent neighbors. Everyone was superior to the Jews; any single person could decide whether a Jew lived or died.

Barbed wire surrounding them, the Jews lived in cities of the damned. And, with bitter irony, everything that befell them seemed to be the work of their own people. The leader of the ghetto was a respected old man; he was surrounded by advisors. They were to transmit German orders to the community. They were in charge of all services: health care, housing, food, law and order. The enemy wanted the victims' humiliation, even their extinction, to look like an internal matter. Tools of the Germans, the Jewish "officials" weren't always up to the job. In Warsaw, in July 1942, Adam Czerniakov committed suicide rather than hand over a higher-than-usual quota of people to be deported to the concentration camp at Treblinka. On the other hand, in Lodz, Chaim Rumkowski operated like the "King of the Jews." His kindly visage shone out from the stamps and money printed in the ghetto. He ended up gassed at Birkenau. So too did many of the Jewish ghetto policemen. Not even the most eager collaborators—an infinitely smaller number than those who played no part in their own people's demise—were spared. For the designers of the "final solution," all Jews were condemned. Even those Jews who were temporarily used by the Nazis, those who thought they were safe, were fooled: their birth certificate was their death certificate.

A Jewish woman holds onto a balcony;
the SS wait for her in the street.

Those Jews who had managed to get "Aryan" documents in order to survive lived under constant threat. Informers tracking them down could recognize them by, among other things, their sad eyes.

Occasionally, the SS would burst into a ghetto and give free rein to their sadistic fantasies. In the Warsaw ghetto, an officer strolled with a dog called "Man," trained to attack the genitals of Jews, whom he called "dogs." Often, bored, the SS would limit themselves to killing a child in front of its mother, a father in front of his children, or random passersby: not for any particular reason, just because they happened to be walking down the street. The next day, the Germans would reassure the Jewish leadership, who in turn would tell the ghetto-dwellers: It won't happen again. The Germans operated on two levels to unsettle the Jews: now a storm, now a period of calm; the two periods alternated and came to resemble each other.

Life soon became unbearable in the seriously overcrowded ghettos, just as the Germans hoped. The Warsaw ghetto was designed to hold 30,000 to 50,000 people; more than 500,000 people were crammed in there. It was a suffocating environment, just like in Lodz and Białystok, Sosnoviec and Lublin, Vilna and Riga. It was physically and mentally impossible to find somewhere to spend a restful hour with friends or family.

And then there was the hunger. The German administration wanted to starve those in the ghettos. To exhaust them. To push them to the edge. To invite death. To make the inhabitants think of death as a liberator.

But the torturers also sought to exploit the Jews in their factories until the last breath. So they told them that work would save them. Anyone with the appropriate documents felt protected. But the documents could change arbitrarily; yesterday's protected became today's condemned. Fear took permanent hold over the minds of those in the ghetto. It was impossible to predict what the enemy would do next.

Weakened by cold, hunger, and lack of space, living in horrendous sanitary conditions, the Jews fell victim to frequent epidemics. These decimated the ghettos as much as the quotas ("actions," in the language of the ghettos) demanded by the Germans for deportation to the extermination camps. In Warsaw, typhus killed tens of thousands of people in just one season.

Naturally, the obstacles were easier to overcome for the healthy: the Germans relied on them. Their physical strength became a virtue. And the danger increased for those less luckily endowed: the sick, the old, the children. Ah, the poor children, those unforgettable children of the ghettos! You could see them in the streets between two "actions," their hands outstretched, their melodious but weakened voices saying: "Mercy, have mercy . . . a little bread . . . mercy . . . ." But back then there was no one on earth below or in heaven above who had mercy on the orphan children of the ghettos.

Among them were some true heroes. At night, they crawled through the barbed-wire fences to the Aryan neighborhoods, risking their lives to bring back a little bread or a few potatoes for their families. Often the SS or Ukrainian guards were waiting for them when they got back. And shot them. The great poet-martyr Itzhak Katzenelson wrote that after the war someone should build a monument to the memory of the little unknown Jewish smuggler.

And yet . . . .

At death's door, the living did the impossible to embrace life. More-or-less legal newspapers brought back

A Jewish man emerges from his hiding place below the floor of a bunker in Warsaw.

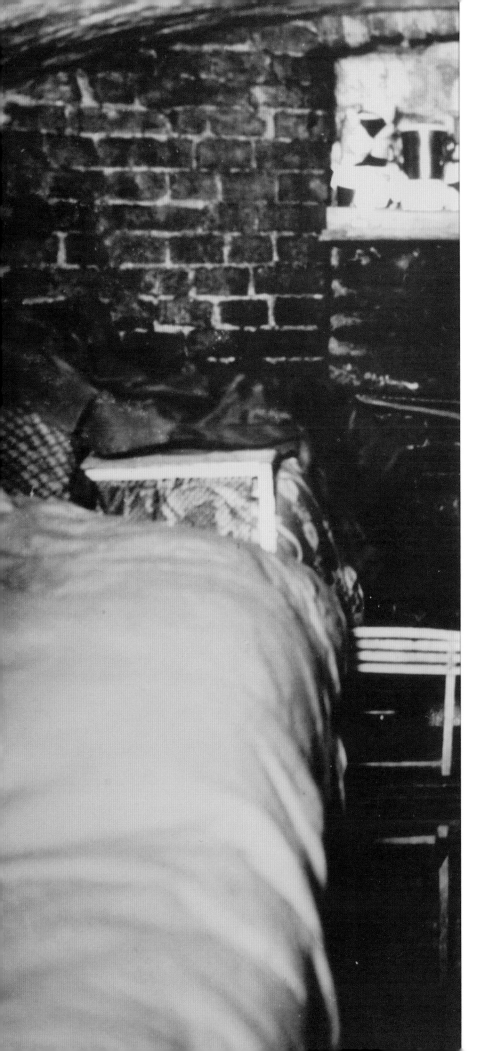

1941   "I held my breath waiting"

The SS men and the Ukrainians, again screaming and hitting us until we all were bleeding, herded us on the run toward the undressing point on the other side of the prison building.

When we turned a corner of the building, I saw a small shed with its door open. As our group was running past the shed I jumped in. I held my breath waiting, but no one had noticed me, and the whole group, including my father and brother and the guards, ran past the shed.

I didn't know if Father or my brother Mietek saw me run into the shed. My heart was beating so loud and fast I could hear it.

I looked around the inside of the shed . . . . In the middle of the ceiling was a two feet by two feet opening to the attic of the shed. Reaching with my hands for the edges of the opening I pulled myself into the attic, and waited. Nobody followed, or went looking for me. Evidently nobody had noticed.

I heard the muffled screams of the SS and Ukrainian guards, and then the cry of the victims in Hebrew: *Shema Israel Adonay Eloheynu Adonay Ehod* (Listen Israel The Lord is Ours, The Lord is One). The ancient Hebrew cry of the persecuted. It was the last cry of the murdered, including my father and Mietek . . . .

Mother kept asking me for details of Mietek and Father again and again. How was the life in the Krzemieniec ghetto? How did the Germans and Ukrainians act against the Jews in the ghetto? How was their health, and did they have enough food? I tried to calm her with invented stories that they were doing well, and that the Germans did not bother the Jews in the ghetto, but I didn't think she fully believed me. She kept asking me the same questions over and over. In view of what was happening in the Warsaw ghetto, and not knowing they both had been killed, she hoped that they would not try to return to Warsaw.

Seeing the horror of the German deportation action in the ghetto, and the danger facing both Mother and me, I kept asking myself why, after escaping from the execution in the jail, I came back to this hell in the Warsaw ghetto. I could have escaped to Romania or Slovakia, which were not that far from the city of Lvov, and yet how could I have left Mother and Mina alone in the Warsaw ghetto?

Adam Boren [Adek Borensztejn],
born 1929, Poland

news—sometimes optimistic, but not always—from the front. The Resistance had ways of letting people know about the dangers closing in on them, but who knew what to believe? In the hospitals, doctors and nurses took care of the sick. The clergy prayed; students studied the Talmud; rabbis blessed marriages—yes, people did get married in the ghettos. And they had their male children circumcised. In this gloomy world, people tried to live something of a normal life. For some, that meant resisting the enemy. Artists sang, musicians played—yes, in that thrown-together place, that bridge toward death, there were quality concerts and artistic programs. In the clandestine schools, teachers taught literature and science. The students received certificates and diplomas. In the Warsaw ghetto, the famous educator Janusz Korczak took care of several hundred orphans who, thanks to him, could sing and observe the holidays. He protected them as best he could, moving heaven and earth to grant them a few moments of happiness. And when, at the final hour, they were taken to the train station and shoved into cattle cars, he refused to abandon them. He could have saved himself: Christian friends begged him to come hide at their houses on the Aryan side. He wanted nothing to do with it. He knew his place was with his children. Together, they arrived at the artificial train station in Treblinka, where the clock always showed the same time: midnight.

We know all of this, and lots of other things besides, thanks to the records witnesses kept. All the ghettos had their chroniclers. Among them were people of all ages. David Flinker was a teenager. In Theresienstadt, children wrote poems that we read as tributes. The teacher Chaim Kaplan hid his journal during an "action." Its last words were: "If they take me away now, what will become of my journal?" The most famous record-keeper was the historian Emmanuel Ringelblum. He created the "Oneg Shabbat"—"joy in the Sabbath"—committee, which had one hundred members. Their job was to gather all the information they could about Jewish life under the occupation. Social activities, religious events, cultural happenings: every member had a beat. Their reports were buried in milk cans and discovered after the liberation. Everything is there. The German policy of deception and entrapment. The moral dilemmas the Jewish Council suffered. The daily bread rations. Medical problems. The behavior of the Jewish police. Of the collaborators. The misery of the masses and the luxury of the elites. The price of bread. The fear. The first news of massacres. The first rumors about the death camp

Jewish children gather together in the Warsaw ghetto.

at Treblinka. The evacuations and occasional escapes. The newspapers of the underground political parties. The calls to resistance.

Because even when they were encircled and walled in by the Germans, an organized resistance inspired young people—not too many, admittedly, but all deeply motivated—in Vilna and Białystok and Warsaw. In Warsaw, the Resistance, present from the beginning, only flowered in the ghetto's last months. The leader of the movement, made up of various groups, was a young Zionist, Mordechai Anielewicz, only twenty-four years old. His assistant Antek Zukerman, even younger, hid on the Aryan side and maintained links to the Communist and Nationalist Polish resistance. His major mission was to find weapons: a pistol was invaluable. The first public operation of the Resistance was the execution of a Jewish collaborator or informer in the service of the Gestapo. Between January and April 1943, the Warsaw ghetto was ruled by the Resistance—but its population had been reduced from 500,000 to 40,000. Of these, 1,200 were active fighters.

The armed rebellion began on April 19—just before Passover—and lasted more than six weeks. It took the SS by surprise: they didn't believe Jews could fight. In fact, the Jews themselves were surprised. When the first Germans fell, the combatants set to dancing out of pride and joy. Perhaps they didn't believe that the enemy was mortal.

Documents from the Resistance in Vilna and Białystok have survived. But most of what is available comes from Warsaw. Posters. Appeals from the commander-in-chief. His letters to his friends outside the ghetto, addressed to the conscience of humankind, will forever be among the most glorious and moving writings of their time. They are full of accusations against those who abandoned them; he insists time and time again that the Jews must preserve their honor in the face of German brutality. The Germans had to resort to air bombing and flamethrowers to burn down the ghetto, both its houses and its underground shelters. In one of them, the headquarters of the revolt at Mila 18, led by Mordechai Anielewicz, the last trapped combatants chose to take their own lives rather than give in to the SS.

Everyone who escaped the flames was sent to Treblinka.

Thousands of Jews are captured and deported during the uprising in the Warsaw ghetto.

ON JANUARY 20, 1942, in a villa in the fancy Berlin neighborhood of Wannsee, the Nazi leaders had met to discuss the Jewish problem. The group, led by Heydrich, decided that fateful day to annihilate the Jewish people. They didn't call it the Holocaust; they called it the Final Solution.

The records of the meeting, read and confirmed by Eichmann at his trial in Jerusalem in 1961, are precise. The document deals with the Jews—all the Jews, eleven million in all, including those still living freely in America. The most important men from all sectors of the Nazi government were there. The mood was serious; the men sipped cognac.

This document—dry and uncomplicated—makes my blood run cold.

And now what was conceived at Wannsee was brought to fruition. Treblinka, Majdanek, Sobibor, Belzec, Chelmno, and Auschwitz. These six places of horror and utter damnation, "death camps," were planned for annihilation, *Vernichtungslager*. These camps were not places where people could live, even by working. They were there to die, victims of an invention of proud German scientists and engineers: the gas chamber. These were death factories.

Truth be told, gas had been used to kill innocent people years before the war began. In 1937, Hitler had ordered his medical service to eliminate the mentally handicapped and people with severe illnesses. Not a single doctor objected. Hundreds and thousands of German men and women had already been murdered in specially equipped clinics. The operation was only stopped when the courageous German bishop von Gallen denounced it from his pulpit in 1941.

But the method was perfected when it came time to kill Jews. This time, no one in Germany protested. Does that mean there was no compassion anywhere? Of course there was. Heinrich Himmler, the all-powerful head of the SS and the Gestapo, had pity: not on the victims, but on the killers. After a day spent observing the

A gas chamber at Majdanek.

Einsatzgruppen in occupied Russia, he became convinced that mowing down people with machine guns could damage the mental health—even the morale—of the murderers (almost all of whose leaders were college-educated). So out of sympathy for the killers he ordered the construction of gas chambers. There, anonymously, they could carry out their task, never having to take their gloves off.

Treblinka: 800,000 dead. Sobibor: 250,000. Majdanek: more than a million. Auschwitz: two million. Never in the history of humankind—whose bloodstained history is full of the most horrendous crimes—had so many people been murdered in such small areas in such a short time.

As much as—if not more than—the triumphs of the human spirit, these monuments of ash blazed through the twentieth century.

Auschwitz—*Oświęcim* in Polish—is located in Upper Silesia. It was made up of three camps: Auschwitz I, Birkenau; Auschwitz II, the central camp; Auschwitz III, Buna-Monowitz, where the prisoners were worked to death for German companies such as I.G. Farben.

Victims were brought to Birkenau at night in sealed cattle cars. They were greeted by strange men in striped pajamas shouting: "Out, everyone out! Leave your things in the train—you'll get them later." But there was no later for people arriving at Auschwitz. The SS shouted the next order: "Men this way, women that way!" Families were beaten into separation. Children often didn't have time to say goodbye to their parents. Pushed by clubs wielded by the SS men, frightened by the barking of their dogs, those in the two lines moved toward the "selection": SS doctors quickly inspected them to send old people, sick people, pregnant women, and small children to one side; the other side was for people chosen to die a slow death from overwork, hunger, and torture. Above, beneath an indifferent sky, gigantic flames from the ovens flashed angrily, signs of the evil still to come.

The gas chambers and the neighboring crematoria were built to SS specifications by private companies. In the spring of 1944, they could

1. Jews from the Lodz ghetto board deportation trains bound for the Chelmno death camp.

2. Children at Auschwitz, wearing adult-size prison jackets, peer through a barbed-wire fence.

3. A warehouse at Auschwitz overflows with clothes taken from prisoners.

1943 "Go to the left, go to the left"

The air is becoming scarcer and scarcer. Huddled in a corner, my legs hurt from being curled up. But standing up or sitting down again is like doing acrobatics. My mother is clutching my backpack tightly, our only piece of luggage. I will find out later that together with our greatest treasures she took my school report cards. You never know. If there will be a school, they will come in very handy. At this moment, what we need are the bare essentials: air, water, and food. Finally the train stops. We hear voices, our door slides open, and with shouts of "Out," they herd us out on the platform for distribution of water. They give us only a few minutes and then the train leaves again . . . . Finally the train stops for good. All the doors open and we get out on the side of a railroad track. I walk alongside my mother and we notice a barbed wire area. Inside of it "march past" haggard beings, with shaved heads, dressed in funny clothes with big blue stripes. The guards reassure us. Rumor has it "those are crazies locked up in this camp."

We continue along the rails and see men who are busy cleaning and repairing them. Suddenly one of them approaches me and walking next to me murmurs quietly: "Watch out, little girl! At the end of the train there is a selection, to the left Life, to the right Death. So watch out and with all your strength dash to the left." I look at him anguished. "And my mother?" The man looks at her. Strange how my mother's hair turned gray recently. He shakes his head without a word and quickly walks away. I realize suddenly that I am the only one who knows what fate awaits us. My thoughts jumble. How can I let everybody know it, without shouting, and without stirring up a panic? I find no solution other than murmuring like one possessed "Go to the left, go to the left." I cannot stop. I repeat these words incessantly and I walk fast to let as many people know as possible. I pull my mother with me without stopping even for an instant . . . . The crowd carries us along and we arrive before the "jury." Two men and one woman stop me, look me over, and push me to the left. Now it's my mother's turn, the seconds seem interminable. They hesitate visibly. Luckily the human stream becomes denser. I dash, I grab my mother's hand and we leave, running for our lives.

Isabelle Choko [born Sztrauch],
born 1927, Poland

"deal with" 12,000 Hungarian Jews every day. Some groups of people went directly from the train platforms to their deaths.

The lucky ones were sent to Auschwitz I or II or III or to the other camps (there were about 1,500) that dotted the map of Poland and Greater Germany. As long as Jews could contribute something to the German war effort, they had the right to live. Every day, though, brought its share of agony and ordeals. Inmates had to withstand the beatings, the forced marches, the starvation diets, the disease, the death, the sadness, the subhuman living standards, and, in winter, the cold. And they had to get used to the smell: the smell of burning flesh that hung over their barracks. SS doctors carried out regular "selections." Those chosen knew what awaited them: they were "leaving for the chimney."

On the entryway to Buchenwald—near Weimar, the city of Goethe—were the words "*Jeden das seine*" ("To each his own"). At Auschwitz II: "*Arbeit macht frei*" ("Work makes you free"), words attributed to the German philosopher Hegel. These camps—like Dachau, Oranienburg, and Mathausen—were international. You could find members of the French and Polish Resistance, Dutchmen and Spaniards, Belgians and Norwegians. And there were Russian and Ukrainian prisoners of war, priests, Gypsies, *Bibelforscher* ("Bible scholars"). The rest of the "death camps" were mainly for Jews.

Auschwitz, like the other camps, was administered by the prisoners themselves, under the close watch of the SS. The most important positions—like that of

1. **Prisoners from Buchenwald** build the Weimar-Buchenwald railroad line.

2. **Two Jewish prisoners** are captured in the Polish forests. They would die in the hands of their captors.

3. **Buchenwald prisoners** taken into the woods await their execution.

"My main responsibility was to look after my dear father"

My next step was to join the *Klempnerei*, a tin-smithing and roofing workshop, which was housed in one third of a long industrial work shed that also held the *Schloserei*, a tool and dye workshop, and the *Electrischeverke*, the electrical section. I had to prove myself to the head of the *Klempnerei*, but doing so was easy enough because of all the experience I had working for Uncle Mottel in Dzialoszyce . . . .

To make sure everything was done properly, we kept checking the roof for leaks; our lives were at stake. We roofed barracks, the prisoners' eating hall, and some administrative buildings. Most of the buildings were without ceilings, but a few of them had attics. It was in one of these that we decided to cut out a hatch in the roof, making a little trap door to enter an attic hiding place. Whenever there were going to be random selections, shootings, or hangings, *Kommandant* Goeth would come to the camp from his villa. As soon as we saw him coming we knew there was going to be trouble so we'd climb up to the roof, appearing as if we were going to do a repair, but then we would disappear into our hiding place.

Whenever I suspected that there was going to be a selection of elderly people or others not working efficiently enough for the slave drivers, I hid Father in the attic. However, since Father was afraid to climb the ladder and hesitant to hide, I arranged a placement for him in the *Birsteingemeindeh* [the brush factory]. My job as *Klempner* gave me access to the different workshops in the camp and I was able to select the most appropriate place for Father. My father learned how to bind brushes and fit in with the mostly religious middle-aged gentlemen who staffed the workshop . . . .

I felt that my main responsibility was to look after my dear father. Now that Father was working in the brush factory, I tried to get him extra rations of soup. One day the *Ordnungsdienst* in charge of the kitchen was having a tryst with his lover. I was able to spy on them from on top of the barracks they used by removing some boards from the roof . . . . It started to rain, and the lovers could not carry on because of water leaking in from my having properly "prepared" the roof. I then walked by conspicuously with a big box of tools strapped to my shoulder and carrying a roll of tarpaper. As soon as the two noticed me, they asked me to fix the leak right away. As a reward, I asked the *Ordnungsdienst* for a soup permit. As the secretary of the kitchen it was he who gave out the soup coupons to the different barracks. What I learned from my brother Willie came in handy. By adding a zero to the one, I could get ten soups.

Joseph E. Tenenbaum, born 1927, Poland

the *Lageraltester*, the camp boss—were reserved for German criminals from German prisons. They wore green triangles. Red triangles ran Buchenwald; they marked political prisoners. Pink triangles were for homosexuals. Jews wore the Star of David. In the hierarchy of the camp, they were the very lowest. Any "eminence" or notable could beat them, punish them, terrorize them, or even kill them without fear of punishment.

At least one witness will never forget what he saw there. Torn from his country, his city, his street, his family, his name, his identity reduced to a number tattooed on his left arm, he found himself tossed into a different universe, in a time outside of time, with its own structures and laws, its philosophers and its theorists, its princes and its thugs. The killers killed; the victims died; the torturers were at the service of Death; their masters were at the service of the devil. Here, the witness discovered a parallel universe, a kind of laboratory designed to dehumanize humans by taking away their dignity, their hope, their reasons for living. The typical Auschwitz Man was the individual who finally lost touch with reality, who lost his individuality, who lost his self, who no longer noticed hunger or thirst or even fear; he no longer thought; he no longer spoke; he no longer listened; he no longer cried; he no longer looked around. Conquered by indifference, he was dead even before his death.

What was it like to live in Auschwitz? An endless experience of nostalgia, suffering, remorse, fear, humiliation. Endless roll calls beneath the rain and the snow. Forced labor. Hunger gnawing at the body and dominating the mind: it was impossible to think of anything else. A little crust of bread or a ladle of soup was the only hope. Some link to humanity—a father, a friend— was indispensable; without something to hold on to,

Prisoners stand together during a roll call at Buchenwald.

people could only throw themselves onto the electrified barbed-wire fences.

But there were things that brought the prisoners together. Rare but inspiring moments: People strengthening each other with words and signs. The dying man offering his ration of bread to his neighbor. The sick man who, after the "selection," bequeathed his "possessions" to a young person he didn't even know. The religious men who prayed together. The Hassid who exhorted them: "For the love of heaven, Jewish brothers, do not abandon hope!"

Don't abandon hope? It wasn't easy.

The most despairing prisoners were the members of the *Sonderkommandos*, the men forced to burn the bodies of people who had been gassed. They often had to stumble over their brothers, their wives, their parents. How they kept their sanity is one of the enduring mysteries of the Holocaust. In the death camps, as in the ghettos, there were some chroniclers who took notes. Written by the light of the crematoria flames, the pages of Zalmen Gradowski and Yehuda-Leib Langfus were discovered in the canteens of Russian soldiers and beneath the mountain of ash at Birkenau.

There was another brilliant, tragic mystery, that of resistance in the death camps. Led mainly by German communists and their allies from the occupied countries, the Resistance operated in Buchenwald, where it protected several hundred children and teenagers. With a few hidden arms, it liberated the camp in April 1945, a few hours before the Americans got there. It was even active in Sobibor and Treblinka, where it helped several hundred people escape—an episode of heroic courage and greatness, retold in books and shown on the screen, that should be studied in every school. In Birkenau, the Resistance destroyed the crematoria with dynamite four Jewish women had smuggled out of their workplace at I.G. Farben. They held their tongues even under torture; they were hanged in the square at Auschwitz.

Auschwitz stands liberated, January 1945.

1945 "What happened at Sobibor"

Explosions were heard ceaselessly from all around immediately followed by rising spurts of earth. It never occurred to me that I was running through the minefield and it seemed to me that the others had also not realized the fact either. The choice was to run or be killed on the spot, and certainly not to fall back into the hands of the Germans, and the leading runners were detonating the mines with their bodies, clearing a way through for those who came after. The distance from the camp fence to the forest in the sector where I was running was more than a kilometer. I ran with all my strength, catching and overtaking everyone. When I felt I had put a fair distance between myself and the camp I stopped for a moment and looked back. Before my eyes spread a most wondrous sight that I couldn't have imagined in my wildest dreams—the whole width of the field, from the camp gates near the railway line to the beginning of Compound One, was filled with hundreds of people running—and the Germans could do nothing to stop them. The machine-gun fire which was directed towards us from the camp was increasing in intensity, but darkness was falling rapidly and from moment to moment people were getting farther and farther away and fewer and fewer were getting hit. Flares illuminated the area close to the camp and tracer-bullets left their brief lines of fire, mostly ineffectively, on into the distance.

So many times we had heard the victims being led to the gas-chambers shouting, in their last moments of life—"Tell the world what the Germans are doing!" "Avenge us!" The words penetrated deep within us and turned themselves into the last will and testimony of the dying. Everyone of us dreamed of fulfilling his obligation to carry out those last wishes but not one of us believed that the wish would become reality.

And yet here it was—we had avenged them. The greatest and worst of the murderers were lying dead, killed by those same knife- and axe-wielding Jews whom they sought to kill. Still less did we believe that any of us would leave that damned camp alive—and yet hundreds succeeded in fleeing that horrendous hell and now they were running into the forests, to freedom. And we would tell the world what happened at Sobibor!

Dov Freiberg, born 1927, Poland

LATER, after the liberation, historians and others tried to make sense of it: How could this tragedy have happened? Why didn't the leaders of the free world take the necessary measures, first to avoid it, then to stop it, or at least slow it down? And there was another vitally important question: What did people know about Auschwitz and Treblinka, in America and throughout the world, and when did they know it? Now we can answer that question with certainty. In Washington and London, in Stockholm and Bern, in the Vatican, people knew more about what was happening than did the Jews themselves.

When the Hungarian Jews arrived in Silesia in May 1944, they had never heard the word "Auschwitz." But at the exact same moment, the most important Allied leaders already knew its gloomy connotation—the Final Solution. In German military reports there were mentions of Auschwitz as early as 1942. That same year, a telegram from Geneva informed the State Department that Hitler's Germany had decided to annihilate the Polish Jews. When the Allies broke the Enigma code, German secrets were revealed in the White House and in 10 Downing Street. The Polish government-in-exile in London filled in the details. A representative of the Polish resistance—Jan Karski—reported it to President Roosevelt and Supreme Court Justice Felix Frankfurter. Two witnesses who had escaped from Auschwitz, Rudolf Vrba and Alfred Wetzler, circulated a highly

1. Survivors in the Bergen-Belsen concentration camp peel potatoes near a wooded area in which corpses are piled, April 1945.

2. Women and children, many of whom are suffering from typhus, huddle together in a barracks at Bergen-Belsen after its liberation, April 1945.

3. A British soldier clears corpses in Bergen-Belsen with a bulldozer, April 1945.

1.

1945 "Hello, hello. You are free."

Then came April 15, 1945. I will never forget that day! It was Sunday, a very hot day. It was strange; nobody was seen outside the barracks. The camp seemed to have been abandoned, almost like a cemetery. I was sitting with the nurses and children, telling them stories. I was desperate. I never believed that we would be free from German slavery, but the miracle happened. Suddenly, we felt the earth tremble; something was moving. We were convinced that the Germans were about to blow up the camp. The children were frightened and crying, and we had a hard time calming them down. We all believed that these were the last moments of our lives. It was 3 P.M. We heard a loud voice repeating the same words in English and in German: "Hello, hello. You are free. We are British soldiers and have come to liberate you." These words still resound in my ears. We ran out of the barracks and saw in the middle of the road a British army car with a loudspeaker on top, going through the camp and repeating the same words over and over again. Within minutes, hundreds of women stopped the car, screaming, laughing, and crying. The British soldier, Captain Derrick Sington, cried with us. It seemed to be a dream. How tragic it was that the great majority did not even realize that we were free because they were too sick to understand what was happening.

Soon the hysteria and the euphoria were over. There was joy, yes. We were free, the gates were open, but where were we to go? The liberation had come too late, not only for the dead but for us living as well. We had lost our families, our friends, our homes. We had no place to go and nobody was waiting for us anywhere. We were alive, yes. We were liberated from death, from the fear of death, but the fear of life started.

Hadassah Rosensaft, born 1912, Poland

detailed report in the Allied capitals. Other information trickled in: not rumors, but facts, photos, firsthand accounts. The leading newspapers and magazines discussed—or whispered about—what was happening: a few lines buried somewhere far from the front page.

In other words, Roosevelt and Winston Churchill knew a great deal, but chose to say—and do—nothing about it. Yes, it is true: they were fighting the most urgent of wars against Hitler and his armies. But at the same time it must be said that the fate of the European Jews did not unduly trouble them. Facts speak for themselves, sadly but irrefutably: England and America's great leaders refused to bomb the railway lines to Birkenau while sealed cattle cars were leading the Hungarian Jews toward certain death.

So when the officers and soldiers of General George Patton's Third Army came into Buchenwald on April 11, 1945, they discovered a hell they had known absolutely nothing about.

When the children with dead eyes and skeletal faces looked at them, all they could do was lower their heads and weep.

Survivors at Dachau celebrate the arrival of American troops.

1945 "Don't you recognize me?"

In June 1945 the British burned down Bergen-Belsen Camp, which was riddled with lice, typhus, and other diseases. The British forced the remaining SS guards to gather the corpses, and using trucks, place them in mass graves. The 13,000 bodies that had been lying about before and shortly after liberation were interred with the use of bulldozers between April 15 and 21, 1945.

Two miles away was an abandoned SS Panzer training school. The British military converted the permanent buildings into a DP camp, and transferred the remaining survivors to it. Many were afraid to ride in the transport trucks provided by their liberators. Their memories of the German method of transport to the death camps was still too vivid in their minds. They preferred to walk, albeit slowly to the new location, and amongst themselves, the survivors called the new camp Hohne. The old name of Bergen-Belsen, which the British still used, was unacceptable because of the horror it invoked.

The first weeks in the new Bergen-Belsen DP camp were occupied with searching for family. The walls of the buildings were plastered with thousands of notices asking for information about individuals from all over Europe. The search for kin, however, was mostly unsuccessful. The Germans had brought slave labor from the farthest reaches of the occupied lands, and the camp resounded with a babble of unfamiliar languages and accents which we could not understand, or even identify. Most of the arrivals from the old camp were inquiring for news of kinsfolk.

People walked around dazedly, some stopping others to ask: "Don't you recognize me?" The question was repeated often, but alas, the search for acquaintances was futile, and locating family was almost impossible. The pain of memory added to the mournful regrets in the despairing answers.

Simon Schweitzer, born 1924, Poland

ONCE THE NIGHTMARE OF THE WAR WAS OVER, the survivors of the Holocaust, still weak, still unable to believe all that had happened, all still wounded, awoke in complete confusion. Those who survived wondered if they were the sole member of their families still alive. Uprooted and disoriented, they did not know what to do with their rediscovered freedom. Go back home to look—with hope beyond hope—for a relative? Should they search there for a keepsake they could cling to? Many made this poignant journey, and so many were disappointed. Their old neighbors, the new occupants of Jewish homes, welcomed them with anger and with hate: "What, you aren't dead?" One Polish girl, eighteen years old, in search of her younger brother, spent weeks in the town of her birth; she preferred to stay with a girlfriend rather than risk encountering familiar ghosts that were surely haunting her former home.

Stumbling out of the camps, the caves, the forests—bereft of their belongings and with no homes to return to—tens of thousands of survivors became "displaced persons." The Allied occupation authorities placed them in camps in Germany and Austria where special agencies of the United Nations took care of them—rather poorly, if we can believe official reports.

In the American zone of occupied Germany, Jewish survivors were badly clothed, badly fed, and too often insensitively treated. Alerted to the situation by President Harry Truman, General Dwight D. Eisenhower saw that the iniquities were immediately addressed. In the British Zone, where adjustments had been made sooner, couples formed, marriages were celebrated. Kindergartens and schools opened their doors. And wherever there were survivors, cultural life reawakened. Theaters, clubs, houses of prayer were formed. Newspapers and books appeared. At the displaced persons camps in Foehrenwald, Bergen-Belsen, and Kassel, visitors were surprised by what they saw: "normal" life where it seemed

1. Members of the Kibbutz Hatichiya Nocham Hachshara dance a *hora* in the Foehrenwald displaced persons camp.

2. Josef Rosensaft, Chairman of the Central Jewish Committee in the British Zone of Germany, addresses thousands of demonstrators at the Bergen-Belsen DP camp during a mass protest against the forced return to Germany of refugees on the *Exodus*.

3. Jewish immigrants, many of them concentration camp survivors, sail to Palestine in March 1946 aboard the *Tel Hai*.

1.

2.

"We are the children of the survivors"

I was born in Bergen-Belsen. That is the essence of my being. My cradle stood only a short distance from the mass graves in which Anne Frank and tens of thousands of other European Jews lie buried anonymously. My parents survived the horrors of Auschwitz; my grandparents did not. I am alive; my brother died in a gas chamber.

More than two thousand Jewish children were born in the displaced persons camp of Bergen-Belsen in Germany between 1945 and 1950. What had been one of the most notorious Nazi concentration camps became a sanctuary of life. Today, those children are adults, scattered throughout the world, with families and careers of their own. Most of us have never met, but we know one another intimately. Together with all the other Jews of our generation whose parents experienced Hitler's Europe, we belong to a special group: We are the children of the survivors of the Holocaust.

Confronting our collective identity has not been without cost. Far too often, it has resulted in an artificial and counterproductive separateness. We do not share in our parents' exclusivity. They went through the Holocaust. We did not. They saw their families and friends murdered. We grew up in comfort and security. We are not survivors in any sense of the term. They, and they alone, are entitled to that designation. Nor do we have any exclusive rights to the survivors' legacy or to the memory of the Holocaust. These belong to the Jewish people and to humankind.

However, while being children of survivors does not give us any privileges, it does impose a far-reaching responsibility. We were given life and placed on earth with a solemn obligation. Our parents survived to bear witness. We, in turn, must be their attestors. Our task is to remind the world of the Holocaust to prevent its recurrence.

We have learned from our parents' experiences that indifference to the suffering of others is in itself a crime. Because of who we are, we constitute a moral force whose voice can have an impact on humankind. We must, both individually and collectively, raise this voice on behalf of all, Jews and non-Jews alike, who are subjected to discrimination and oppression, or who are threatened by annihilation, anywhere in the world. And we may never be passive, or allow others to be passive, in the face of oppression, for we know only too well that the ultimate consequence of apathy and silence was embodied forever in the flames of Auschwitz and the mass graves of Bergen-Belsen.

Menachem Z. Rosensaft, born 1948,
Bergen-Belsen DP camp, Germany

ACKNOWLEDGMENTS

I wish to acknowledge the generous assistance of Menachem Rosensaft, director and editor in chief of the Holocaust Survivors' Memoirs Project, for his help in photo research and in securing the testimonies of survivors that appear in these pages. And of course I wish to thank the survivors, whose memoirs are excerpted here, for bearing witness.

—E.W.

A NOTE ABOUT THE AUTHOR

Elie Wiesel is the author of more than forty books, including his unforgettable international best-sellers *Night* and *A Beggar in Jerusalem*, winner of the Prix Médicis. He has been awarded the Presidential Medal of Freedom, the United States Congressional Gold Medal, and the French Legion of Honor with the rank of Grand Cross. In 1986, he received the Nobel Peace Prize. He is Andrew W. Mellon Professor in the Humanities and University Professor at Boston University. He lives with his wife, Marion, in New York City.

IMAGE CREDITS

Endsheets: A memorial candle burns on the railroad tracks at Birkenau. Michael St. Maur Sheil/CORBIS

All images listed below are courtesy of the United States Holocaust Memorial Museum, and credited to the following:

Front Cover: Robert Waisman

Back Cover: (top left) Israel Government Press Office; (middle left) National Archives; (bottom left) Bayerische Staatsbibliothek

Page 1: Archiwum Akt Nowych

Page 3: Muzeum Okregowe Konin

Page 4: Israel Government Press Office

Pages 6-7: (clockwise) Ester Ajzen Lewin; Eva Rosenbaum Abraham-Podietz; Gavra Mandil

Page 8: Norman Salsitz

Pages 10-11: Leo & Edith Cove

Page 13: Debra Gierach

Pages 14-15: Bayerische Staatsbibliothek

Page 17: Yad Vashem Photo Archives

Page 19: American Jewish Joint-Distribution Committee

Pages 20-21: Louis Gonda

Page 23: National Archives

Pages 24-25: State Archives of the Russian Federation

Pages 26-27: National Archives

Pages 28-29: Archiwum Panstwowego Muzeum na Majdanku

Pages 30-31: (clockwise) National Museum of American Jewish History; National Archives; Belarussian State Archive of Documentary Film and Photography

Pages 32-33: (clockwise) Gedenkstaette Buchenwald; Archiwum Akt Nowych; Robert A. Schmuhl

Pages 34-35: Robert A. Schmuhl

Pages 36-37: Philip Vock

Pages 38-39: (left and bottom right) Imperial War Museum; (top right) Hadassah Bimko Rosensaft

Pages 40-41: (both) National Archives

Pages 42-43: (top and right) Alex Knobler; (bottom left) Yad Vashem Photo Archives

Pages 44-45: Robert Waisman

Page 48: Frederic Brenner

TESTIMONIAL CREDITS

Margaret Lambert

From an unpublished manuscript, untitled.

Eve Nussbaum Soumerai

From the unpublished manuscript *Holding On . . .* ; another version of this excerpt appears in a book of essays tentatively entitled *A Voice from the Holocaust*, to be published by Greenwood Press.

Jane Lipski [Jadzia Szpigelman]

From the unpublished manuscript *My Escape into Prison (and Other Memories of a Stolen Youth)*.

Adam Boren [Adek Borensztejn]

From the unpublished manuscript *Against All Odds: Journey Through Inferno*.

Isabelle Choko [born Sztrauch]

From the unpublished manuscript *Ma Première Vie*.

Joseph E. Tenenbaum

From the unpublished manuscript *Building from the Rubble*.

Dov Freiberg

From the manuscript *Sobibor*, privately published in Hebrew.

Hadassah Rosensaft

From the unpublished manuscript *Yesterday*.

Simon Schweitzer

From the manuscript *Simon's Quest*, to be published in German by Büchergilde Gutenberg.

Menachem Z. Rosensaft

From "I Was Born in Bergen-Belsen," published in *Second Generation Voices: Reflections by Children of Holocaust Survivors and Perpetrators* (New York: Syracuse University Press, 2001).

The survivors' testimonies in this book are excerpted from memoirs gathered by the Holocaust Survivors' Memoirs Project of the World Jewish Congress. They will be published by the United States Holocaust Memorial Museum pursuant to a grant from Random House, Inc.